A SPIRIT OF
EXCELLENCE

IS IT WITHIN YOU?

RICHARD ROBERTS

Unless otherwise noted, scripture quotations are taken from the New King James Version® Copyright © 1982 by Thomas Nelson. Used by permission. All rights reserved.

Scripture quotations marked AMP taken from the Amplified® Bible (AMPC), Copyright © 1954, 1958, 1962, 1964, 1965, 1987 by The Lockman Foundation. Used by permission. lockman.org.

Scripture quotations marked CEV are from the Contemporary English Version Copyright © 1991, 1992, 1995 by American Bible Society, Used by Permission.

Scripture quotations marked ESV are from the ESV® Bible (The Holy Bible, English Standard Version®), copyright © 2001 by Crossway, a publishing ministry of Good News Publishers. Used by permission. All rights reserved.

Scripture quotations marked GNT are from the Good News Translation in Today's English Version- Second Edition Copyright © 1992 by American Bible Society. Used by Permission.

Scriptures marked KJV are taken from the King James Version of the Bible. Public domain.

Scripture quotations marked MSG are taken from The Message, copyright © 1993, 2002, 2018 by Eugene H. Peterson. Used by permission of NavPress. All rights reserved. Represented by Tyndale House Publishers.

Scripture quotations marked NIV are taken from the Holy Bible, New International Version®, NIV®. Copyright © 1973, 1978, 1984, 2011 by Biblica, Inc.™ Used by permission of Zondervan. All rights reserved worldwide. www.zondervan.com. The "NIV" and "New International Version" are trademarks registered in the United States Patent and Trademark Office by Biblica, Inc.™

Scripture quotations marked TLB are taken from The Living Bible, copyright © 1971 by Tyndale House Foundation. Used by permission of Tyndale House Publishers, Carol Stream, Illinois 60188. All rights reserved.

Copyright © 2023
By Richard Roberts
Tulsa, Oklahoma

ISBN 978-1-7346612-9-3

Published by Oral Roberts Evangelistic Association,
DBA Richard Roberts Ministries • PO Box 2187 • Tulsa, OK 74102-2187

All rights reserved.

Printed in the United States of America

Table of Contents

Chapter 1
To Soar Like an Eagle 9

Chapter 2
Choosing Excellence 15

Chapter 3
Faith over Fear 19

Chapter 4
Prayer—The Key to Excellence 25

Chapter 5
The Power of Believing Prayer 29

Chapter 6
Distractions and Detractors 35

Chapter 7
Embracing the 2 D's of Excellence—Discipline
and Diligence 41

Chapter 8
Reigning in Life and Triumphing over Adversity 49

Chapter 9
Loyalty Brings Reward 55

Chapter 10
Free, Indeed 59

Chapter 11
For Such a Time as This... 61

Summary... 67

DEDICATION

I dedicate this book to my beloved wife, Lindsay,
whose faithful and steadfast love and support
has strengthened me beyond measure.

INTRODUCTION

You are unique. You are irreplaceable. There is no one else like you in the whole world. Nobody has your DNA. You are special to God, and His plan for you is for good and not for evil.

His desire is for you to excel in every area of your life…to be above and not beneath…to be the head and not the tail… blessed when you come in and blessed when you go out.

And if you will believe it and set your faith on it, every day you can know and believe that great things are coming your way!

Richard Roberts

CHAPTER 1

To Soar Like an Eagle

Excellence is to do a common thing in an uncommon way.

BOOKER T. WASHINGTON

I have always been fascinated by the majestic eagle. Eagles have microscopic and telescopic vision and are able to see both close up as well as great distances. Their eyesight is 20/4 or 20/5, around five times better than that of humans, meaning they can actually see an animal the size of a rabbit up to three miles away!

Eagles build their nests on cliffs or in the tallest trees. They have a God-given way of setting their wings when storms come and are able to rise above the clouds and out of the dangerous weather.

These powerful creatures are regarded in the Bible as a sign of mercy and divine power. And it's no wonder that God used them as examples of how we humans can overcome obstacles when we trust Him with our lives and have faith in His Word. Faith in God enables us to soar high like the eagle.

When God delivered Israel from four hundred years of slavery in Egypt, He said that He carried them "on eagles' wings" (Exodus 19:4). And you and I were created in His image, designed for high flight, as eagles in the kingdom of God.

Becoming Who You Believe You Are

Unfortunately, there are many today like the little eaglet who fell from the nest and was separated from his mother.

A farmer noticed the little bird and captured it. When he got back home, he put something on its wings so it could not learn to fly and turned it loose to roam the barnyard.

It wasn't long until the eaglet began to act like the chickens, scratching and pecking for food.

This bird that was created to soar in the sky seemed satisfied to live in the barnyard with the chickens.

Then one day, as he was clawing and clucking and digging and flapping, a huge shadow passed over him in the heavens. When he looked up, he was startled by the sight of the majestic creature soaring high above him on the wind currents. Its wingspread was so broad that it seemed to fill the sky.

He looked over at one of his chicken buddies, nudged him, pointed up in the air and said, "What's that?"

The chicken shrugged its tiny little wings and said, "That's the mighty eagle. And, oh, see what an enormous wingspread it has! See how proudly it soars through the heavens. But don't pay any attention to it. You're just a chicken. You'll never be able to fly like that."

The little eaglet stared up into the sky for a few more seconds, then dropped his head and went back to clawing, digging and scratching in the dirt, never suspecting that he, too, was created by God to soar through the vast expanse of the sky.

Friend, it's so true that we become who we believe we are.

So, allow me to remind you of just who you are when your true identity is in Jesus Christ...

In Christ...

- You are dead to sin but alive to God and free from the law of sin and death (Romans 6:11 & 8:2).

- Nothing can separate you from God's love (Romans 8:39).

- You are an heir of God (Galatians 3:26).

- You have the hope of glory and the promise of life (Colossians 1:27 & 2 Timothy 1:1).

- You are victorious (1 Corinthians 15:57).

Second Peter 1:3-4 says... *His divine power has given to us all things that pertain to life and godliness, through the knowledge of Him who called us by glory and virtue, by which have been given to us exceedingly great and precious promises, that through these you may be partakers of the divine nature.*

In Christ, you have His divine and excellent nature.

The little eagle had been looking down for so long that he did not know what it was like to spread his wings and fly. Now, I don't know about you, but that's not the way I want to live my life. I don't want to be like those chickens, always looking down in the dirt, totally defeated and downtrodden.

You see, you and I, like the mighty eagle, were meant to fly, to soar above the storms of life. So, the message of this story is very clear...

Don't let anyone tell you that you can't rise and soar to your highest potential. Don't let anyone convince you that you cannot develop the gifts that God has placed within you. Believe what God says about you.

Your Spiritual DNA

There is a spark of divine excellence inside you that is waiting to explode into its full and brilliant potential.

You are the divine creation of an excellent God. You have been created only a little lower than the angels and you were redeemed by the royal blood of Jesus. You were created in His image and in His likeness. You have His spiritual DNA.

In Psalm 16:3, God declares, *As for the saints who are on the earth, they are the excellent ones, in whom is all my delight.*

I tell you, it's God's will for you to achieve excellence... excellence in every area of your life...in your spirit, your mind, will and emotions, your body, your finances, your family and in every other area. In fact, 3 John 2 tells us that it's God's highest wish for us to be in health and to prosper—to *excel*—even as our soul prospers.

So, don't be satisfied with the status-quo; don't settle for the mediocre. Don't let a fear of change cause you to just park yourself, thinking you can never advance any further. Instead, continue to push forward, to study, to grow and to learn and to gain more understanding and knowledge of God's will for you and His ways of doing and being, as Proverbs 4:5 AMP instructs... *Get* [skillful and godly] *wisdom! Acquire understanding* [actively seek spiritual discernment, mature comprehension, and logical interpretation]! *Do not forget nor turn away from the words of my mouth.*

Second Peter 1:5 also tells us, *And beside this, giving all diligence, add to your faith virtue.* The word *virtue* here can be translated as "excellence."

Friend, God has already put an excellent spirit inside you. It's your choice to add that excellence to your faith and to unleash all your potential. Through faith, God can do in you and through you all He desires so you can become all He created you to be.

Second Peter 1:5-9 goes on to say, ... *add to your faith virtue, to virtue knowledge, to knowledge self-control, to self-control perseverance, to perseverance godliness, to godliness brotherly kindness, and to brotherly kindness love. For if these things are yours and abound, you will be neither barren nor unfruitful in the knowledge of our Lord Jesus Christ.*

Look to almighty God, the One in whom "all things are possible" (Matthew 19:26). And when you do, you, too, can begin to soar high as the majestic eagle.

CHAPTER 2

Choosing Excellence

*And whatever you do, do it heartily, as to the Lord and not to men,
knowing that from the Lord you will receive the reward of the
inheritance; for you serve the Lord Christ.*

COLOSSIANS 3:23-24

As we established in chapter one, because God put His excellent spirit inside each of us, developing and exercising a spirit of excellence in life is a matter of choice.

But, what does it really mean to have a spirit of excellence or to have an excellent spirit? How do we develop habits of excellence?

Well, some of the synonyms for the words *excellence* or *excellent* are exceptional...first-rate...admirable...distinction and quality.

Notice, nowhere in the list above is the word "perfect."

Although we should always strive to be that person of excellent spirit, excellence does not necessarily equate with perfection. Only Jesus was perfect and without sin, and it's His strength within us that is made perfect in our weakness (2 Corinthians 12:9).

God, who created the heavens and the earth and everything in it, is a mighty and excellent Creator. Everything He does is first-class.

Psalm 8:1 KJV declares, *How excellent is thy name.* Job 37:23 also tells us, *He is excellent in power, and in judgment.*

In Genesis 1:26, when God created man in His image and His likeness, He put within us the seeds of His divine excellence. If you don't believe it, just look at the history of the human race. It's marked by great achievements made by ordinary people—people just like you and me—who chose excellence in spite of the overwhelming odds they were up against.

For example, it's believed that Albert Einstein had dyslexia when he was growing up, which would have made studying difficult for him. Yet one of his greatest gifts to mankind was the revolutionary theory of relativity!

And it also might interest you to know that Thomas Edison failed thousands of times in his efforts to invent the first light bulb. Someone once said to him, "Mr. Edison, weren't you dejected when you failed six thousand times?"

"No," he replied, "now I know six thousand things that don't work!"

We know from the history books that even though as a child Sir Walter Scott was afflicted with polio which left him lame, he went on to become a noted historian, author and writer/poet.

Rosa Parks, a small child who was often bullied in school and who suffered from poor health and chronic tonsillitis, started a national movement for black equality when she refused to obey a then, "Jim Crow law" of racial segregation in the South by not giving up her seat on the bus to a white person and moving to the back of the bus. Her courage and fortitude, her excellent spirit, on that day and for the rest of her life, made her the first woman and the second African-American person to lie in honor in the Capitol upon her death.

Theodore Roosevelt, one of our most renowned American presidents, was stricken with asthma. However, his legacy of forestry, game reserves, national parks and monuments are found across America.

Helen Keller grew up blind and deaf, but later achieved much success as an author and activist and changed the perceptions of many regarding the deaf and blind communities.

Ruth Bader Ginsburg survived many trials and tribulations in life, including the loss of her mother the day before her high school graduation. That didn't stop her from becoming a great advocate against gender discrimination in the workplace, successfully arguing six landmark cases before the Supreme Court and eventually being appointed to serve as a Justice in that great Court for twenty-seven years.

And, let's not forget Todd Beamer and the other brave passengers of Flight 93 who chose excellence in deciding to do what they could to stop the terrorists on 9/11, knowing that decision would most likely end in their deaths.

How were all these feats and accomplishments—and so many more through the ages not published here—possible? *It's possible because these men and women chose to be excellent, regardless of physical limitations, societal pressures and restrictions, or fear!*

Now, of course, none of the people mentioned above were perfect and some were most likely not living their lives to please the Lord. Yet, because they chose to let their excellent spirits dictate how they overcame obstacles and negative circumstances in their lives, God honored that spark of excellence already inside them and they achieved much.

However, you and I, as born-again believers, are encouraged by the apostle Paul in Colossians 3:24... *And whatever you do, do it heartily, as to the Lord and not to men, knowing that from the Lord you will receive the reward of the inheritance; for you serve the Lord Christ.*

When you exercise your excellent spirit that is within you, you are opening up yourself to receive God's favor, you're blessing your fellow man, and you're bringing glory to God.

Let's determine today to cultivate an excellent spirit.

CHAPTER 3

Faith over Fear

Let no one despise your youth, but be an example to the believers in word, in conduct, in love, in spirit, in faith, in purity.

1 TIMOTHY 4:12

In the Bible, we learn of many people who had excellent spirits. In this book, I will be highlighting the life of Daniel, while including accounts of other outstanding lives of excellence in the mix. Let's look at a few of them and see what can be learned from their examples.

Daniel 6:3 declares, *Then this Daniel was preferred above the presidents and princes, **because an excellent spirit was in him**.* This same chapter also tells us about Daniel's amazing faithfulness and trust in God.

You may recall the account of Daniel in the lions' den and how he prayed to God to deliver him from the hungry lions. But there was much more to Daniel than just this famous story...more we can learn from him and how he chose to live a life of excellence.

You see, Daniel was an extraordinary young man of faith, and even though he was a captive in the land of Babylon, his excellent spirit caused him to be noticed by King Darius and he was groomed, trained and eventually promoted to the prominent position of the king's second-in-command. Naturally, that decision provoked the jealousy of many of the other officials, so they immediately began to look for a way to discredit Daniel and a way to rob him of his credibility, searching high and low for a way to trip him up!

The Bible says that the men couldn't find any fault in Daniel. He was trustworthy because he was neither corrupt nor negligent (v. 4).

But then they remembered that he got down on his knees three times a day and prayed to the Lord God of Israel. As soon as they remembered Daniel's dedicated prayer life, they said to each other, "That's it! That's the way we can discredit him!" So, they went straight to the king and began to appeal to the king's ego, saying, "O king, there's nobody like you in heaven or on earth. We appreciate your kingly presence so much that we want you to sign a decree stating that if any person prays a prayer to anyone except you, O great and mighty King, they shall be cast into a den of hungry lions." Sadly, the king was seduced by their flattery, and he signed that terrible decree into law (See Daniel 6:6-9.)

Suddenly, Daniel found himself in a world of trouble
(more about Daniel in a later chapter.)

Now, doesn't this sound like what sometimes happens in our own lives, too? We're rolling along, living our lives the best way we know how and doing our best to abide by what we understand God wants for our lives, and then... Wham! The rug is pulled out from under us!

No Bed of Roses

We are not promised that this Christian life will be trouble-free. Jesus Himself said in John 16:33 that in this life we would have trouble and trials. And in 2 Timothy 3:12 it says... *All who desire to live godly in Christ Jesus will suffer persecution.*

Every phone call you receive may not be wonderful news. You may not be well received in every place you go. Not everyone you meet will be fascinated by your wit and charm.

However, trouble is not a sign that God has forgotten you. It's just a reminder that though we are not "of this world," we are in it. And according to John 10:10, the enemy of our soul (Satan) wants to steal, kill and destroy everything good in our lives. He continually roams the earth as a roaring lion looking for those he can devour (1 Peter 5:8).

But you and I have God's excellent spirit inside us and in the second part of John 16:33, which I quoted above, Jesus says... *Be of good cheer; I have overcome the world!* Also, 1 John 4:4 reminds us, ...*He* [Jesus] *who is in you is greater than he who is in the world.* Believers in Jesus, through the indwelling of the Holy Spirit, have that same overcoming ability. In fact, 2 Corinthians 2:14 assures us that we can give thanks to God, for He always causes us to triumph in Christ!

Let's look at some more examples in the Bible from whom we can take encouragement from in this matter of excellence.

Weathering the Storms of Life

Remember this account of Jesus and His disciples in Mark chapter 4 as they crossed the Sea of Galilee? A great wind came across the sea and began to beat against their ship with a deadly force! Fearing for their lives, they must have wished they had never tried to cross over in the first place! But Jesus had said to them, "Let us cross over" (Mark 4:35 NIV). And right in the middle of doing God's will, they ran head on into a violent storm and nearly drowned until Jesus saved the day!

I tell you, the storms of life will always be brewing somewhere on the horizon. Someone may be jealous or envious of you. Someone may try to discredit you, speak unkindly to you or repeat untrue things about you. But the Bible says in 1 Peter 3:15-16...*Always be ready to give a defense to everyone who asks you a reason for the hope that is in you, with meekness and fear; having a good conscience, that when they defame you, as evildoers, those who revile your good conduct in Christ may be ashamed.*

The storms of life will also clarify either the excellent spirit within you or show you where it may be lacking.

And... Don't blame God when the winds and waves of life try to overtake you. Put the blame where it belongs...on your adversary, Satan, the devil! He's the one who only comes to steal, kill and destroy. Jesus came that you may have life, and that more abundantly (John 10:10).

Believe me, I know this to be so true in my own life. I have faced many trials, tests and problems. So many obstacles have been thrown in my path and in the path of my family members and in our ministry. And sometimes, I felt like I would never recover...but I did. And so can you! Because God is faithful to His Word. He's never left me or forsaken me. And,

I don't get special favor just because I'm an evangelist! God does not play favorites. What He's done for me, He can do the same for you as you trust and obey Him.

CHAPTER 4

Prayer—The Key to Excellence

Commit your work to the Lord, and your plans will be established.

PROVERBS 16:3 ESV

As Daniel continued his daily prayer vigil, the news of his so-called disloyalty finally reached King Darius. The king realized how he had been cruelly manipulated by his advisors. But he knew that the law of the Medes and the Persians would not allow anyone—*not even the king himself*—to reverse the decree. It crushed him to think about that special young man being cast alive into a den of roaring lions, and he spent the rest of that day trying to figure out a way to rescue him. The king's advisers were quick to remind him that no decree or edict that the king issues could be changed. So, alas, the king had to give the command to have Daniel brought forth and thrown in, but he said to Daniel, "May your God, whom you serve, continually rescue you!"

A stone was even placed over the mouth of the den, and the king sealed it with his signet ring so that Daniel couldn't escape. Then the king returned to his palace, distraught and unable to sleep that night.

At first light the next morning, the king leaped out of bed and ran to the lions' den, crying, "Daniel, has your God been able to rescue you?"

Daniel answered, "My God sent his angel, and he shut the mouths of the lions. They have not hurt me, because I was found innocent in his sight."

The king was overjoyed and gave orders for Daniel to be lifted out of the lions' den. No wound was found on him because he had trusted in his God.

After having the false accusers of Daniel thrown into the lions' den, he then issued a new decree...

"In every part of my kingdom people must fear and reverence the God of Daniel" (Daniel 6:13-26).

Now, let's go back for a moment and examine what Daniel had done to develop an excellent spirit which helped him rise to the test...

Prayer—Your "Go-to" or Your "Last Resort?"

As a captive in a foreign land, Daniel could have just accepted his fate and lived in defeat. But, he *chose* to continue living his life in a way that would honor God.

The Bible says that Daniel was a man of prayer. Three times a day he fell on his knees and faithfully prayed to God (See Daniel 6:10). His diligence and strong prayer life helped him to develop the excellent spirit inside him.

A SPIRIT OF EXCELLENCE | 27

Now, let me ask you...

Are you a person of prayer? Do you routinely seek the Lord with all of your heart? Or do you only pray when you get into some terrible jam?

I remember a young man I once knew who was extremely faithful in his prayer life. In 1966, when I enrolled as a freshman at the University of Kansas, I shared a dormitory room with this young man. He was a Muslim from Saudi Arabia. And five times a day, he knelt down on his prayer rug and prayed. EVERY day, no matter what! Every time I think about his dedicated prayer life, the thought flashes through my mind, *If he could pray like that, how much more should we who believe in the Lord Jesus Christ be faithful to lift our hands and pray to God?*

I often say, "Much prayer, much power, little prayer, little power, no prayer, no power."

I believe in the power of prayer.

Abraham and Moses prayed...the prophets of the Old Testament prayed...King David prayed. Mary, the mother of Jesus, prayed...the apostle Paul prayed and all of Jesus' disciples prayed. Jesus Himself prayed to the Father and shared examples with His disciples of how to pray. (See Matthew chapter 6.)

And you and I are called to pray, too... *Be anxious for nothing, but in everything by prayer and supplication, with thanksgiving, let your requests be made known to God* (Philippians 4:6).

We are to pray when times are good and when times are not so good (2 Timothy 4:2). We are to pray over our nation and our leaders (1 Timothy 2:1-2). We are to pray over our families, our finances, and our health (James 5:16).

We are to pray for ourselves, sharing with God the sincere desires of our heart and delighting in Him. And when we do, He promises in Psalm 37:4 that He will give us those desires.

The apostle James encourages us to... *pray for one another, that you* [we] *may be healed. The effective, fervent prayer of a righteous man avails much* (James 5:16).

And, when we pray about situations or circumstances that are seemingly out of our control or through no fault of our own, we must remember that our battle is not a battle in the flesh; it's not with people. The Bible tells us in Ephesians 6:12 that *we do not wrestle against flesh and blood, but against principalities, against powers, against the rulers of the darkness of this age, against spiritual hosts of wickedness in the heavenly places.*

You know, many spiritual strongholds have been built by those who oppose God, Christianity, and all that we stand for and believe in. But the good news is we can come against those strongholds in prayer... *For though we walk in the flesh* [as mortal men], *we are not carrying on our* [spiritual] *warfare according to the flesh and using the weapons of man. The weapons of our warfare are not physical* [weapons of flesh and blood]. *Our weapons are divinely powerful for the destruction of fortresses. We are destroying sophisticated arguments and every exalted and proud thing that sets itself up against the [true] knowledge of God* (2 Corinthians 10:3-5 AMP).

I encourage you to develop and keep an attitude of prayer always, making it an integral and routine part of your life. As it did for Daniel, prayer will sustain you and uphold you in the trials of life.

CHAPTER 5

The Power of Believing Prayer

And whatever you do in word or deed, do all in the name of the Lord Jesus, giving thanks to God the Father through Him.

COLOSSIANS 3:17

I really don't believe I can stress enough the importance of a consistent prayer life in someone who wants to show forth an excellent spirit.

Perhaps one of the most incredible stories in the Bible about a man who was faithful in his prayer life is the story of the prophet Elijah. (See 1 Kings 17 and 18.)

Elijah was a man whose prayers shook the nation of Israel and caused the king and queen to try to kill him. Let me share with you a moving scene from Elijah's life, at a time when Israel was completely backslidden.

You see, the wicked King Ahab and his wife, Jezebel, had

led the people astray by worshiping idols and offering sacrifices to gods of wood and stone. So, the Lord commanded Elijah to give the king a warning: "It's not going to rain until I say so." And when Elijah prayed for God to shut up the heavens, *no rain fell for over three and a half years!* **What an earthshaking word of prophecy!**

As the crops began to fail without water, King Ahab's spies scoured the countryside, looking for the prophet. No matter how relentlessly they searched for him, every lead came to a dead end!

Then one day the Lord told Elijah to go back to Israel and ask that all the people, plus the prophets of Baal and the prophets of Asherah, meet him on Mount Carmel.

Elijah stood before those heathen idol worshipers and said… "How long are you going to waver between two opinions?" If the Lord is God, follow him, but if Baal is god, follow him." And then Elijah gave this order, "Get two bulls for us. Let them choose one for themselves, and let them cut it into pieces and put it on the wood but not set fire to it. I will prepare the other bull and put it on the wood but not set fire to it. Then, you call on the name of your god, and I will call on the name of the Lord. *The god who answers by fire, he is God"* (See 1 Kings 18:22-24)!

All day long, those false prophets of Baal cried out to their god, shouting and slashing themselves with knives, as was their custom. They cried out from morning until noon, **but no one answered.**

While the false prophets ranted and raved around the altar, I can just imagine Elijah standing there with his hands on his hips, staring at them. The Bible says Elijah mocked them, saying, "Cry aloud, for he is a god; either he is musing or he has gone aside or he is on a journey, or perhaps he is asleep and must be awakened." Then about sunset, the prophet of the Lord had seen enough, and said, "Step aside."

First, he called for someone to bring him water, which he poured over the bull that he had laid upon the altar. Next, he told his helpers to dig a trench around the altar, and he doused the bull with more water until it filled the trench and began to run over the sides. Then he soaked everything around the altar with water so the people would know beyond a shadow of a doubt that God was sending His fire to consume Elijah's sacrifice!

I want you to notice that the prophet of the Lord did not mutilate himself with knives. He didn't strike his body with blunt instruments. He didn't perform any kind of perverse ritual. **He simply prayed!**

He lifted his voice to the Lord and said, *"Let it be known this day that you are God in Israel. Hear me, O Lord, hear me"* (1 Kings 18:36-37).

Then, like a bolt of lightning, the fire of God came streaking down from heaven and consumed his sacrifice, *licking up the water in the trench which surrounded the altar!* **What a dramatic answer to Elijah's prayers!**

And when all the people saw it, thy fell on their faces and said, *The Lord, He is God!* Elijah called for all the false prophets to be seized and killed. Not one escaped!

I tell you, when I have a need in my life, I want someone like Elijah to pray for me! What about you?

Pray a Tent Prayer

I remember when our children were growing up and one of them became ill, Lindsay would ask my dad, Oral Roberts, to pray a "tent prayer" for them. And I knew exactly what she meant when she said it! You see, when I was a boy, I walked the prayer lines inside those great crusade tents alongside my father. And when it came to praying for the sick, he was a man on a mission from God.

So many times, I watched as he laid his hands on people and prayed. At times he almost became violent in his praying! Why? Because he was filled with such a holy hatred for sickness and disease that it seemed as if he wanted to reach down inside the person and physically pull the sickness out!

Friend, when Oral Roberts prayed for you, you knew you'd been prayed for! It was almost electrifying! You talk about the power of God!

My dad prayed so many "tent prayers" for so many people—nearly two million of them over the years of his ministry! And God greatly used him as an anointed instrument through whom His power flowed.

That's what Lindsay meant when she asked for a tent prayer. She wanted a heaven-reaching, hell-shaking, Holy Spirit-filled, prayer! That's the kind of prayers my dad prayed, and I believe it's the kind Elijah prayed also.

Now, your prayers don't have to be said in such a dramatic way as Elijah's were. You don't have to call down fire from heaven to get God to respond to you. Prayer is simply talking to God with the desires of your heart and then listening for His answers. He's not concerned with how loudly you pray but the sincerity with which you pray. He doesn't see as man sees; He looks on the heart (1 Samuel 16:7). And His answers might come in a variety of ways…through revelation of scripture, through a sermon or teaching or through the counsel of a wise friend. And, because we have the Holy Spirit living inside us, we can also sometimes hear God's "still, small voice" as He leads and guides.

And as you and I go forth into this world—a world of hurting and spiritually lost people—we should be increasingly a "people of prayer." God's Word says in 1 Thessalonians 5:17 KJV to "pray without ceasing." That doesn't mean God expects you to be on your knees 24/7 in prayer. It means to always be in an attitude of prayer.

Let me say it again... "Much prayer, much power...little prayer, little power...no prayer, no power."

CHAPTER 6

Distractions and Detractors

It's hard to be a diamond when you live in a rhinestone world.

DOLLY PARTON

Nehemiah is another example in the Bible of a man with an excellent spirit.

You see, Nehemiah was the one who wanted to take on the task of rebuilding the broken-down walls of Jerusalem.

If you recall the background of this story, King Nebuchadnezzar had conquered the city of Jerusalem, smashed the walls with battering rams, and burned the city with fire. Then he kidnapped Israel's finest young men and women, making them captives in the land of Babylon. (See 2 Chronicles 36:17-20.)

When Nebuchadnezzar's legions trampled the walls of Jerusalem, it made the city vulnerable to its enemies and a laughingstock in the eyes of its neighbors! In those days, it was considered a terrible disgrace for the walls of a city to be in such a state of disrepair.

Many years later, Nehemiah was still living in exile in Babylon and one day, he inquired about the conditions back in Jerusalem. He was overcome with grief when he heard that the walls were still in shambles. All that remained of Jerusalem's former glory was charred rubble. The Bible says that Nehemiah was so upset by the news that he wept and mourned and refused to eat for several days. (See Nehemiah 1:2-4.)

Nehemiah served as the king's cup bearer and so had access to the king. He requested to be sent back to Judah to rebuild the walls, and the king gave him permission to go.

When Nehemiah returned to Jerusalem, he proclaimed to the people, *"You know full well the tragedy of our city; it lies in ruins and its gates are burned. Let us rebuild the wall of Jerusalem and rid ourselves of this disgrace"* (Nehemiah 2:17 TLB).

After Nehemiah had shared his plans with the city magistrates, the Bible says, *"They strengthened their hands for this good work"* (Nehemiah 2:18 KJV). In other words, they prepared themselves to do the work God had called them to do. No doubt, they assembled their tools and equipment, lumber and supplies, mortar and stone, and whatever else they would need to reconstruct the walls.

Nehemiah 3 tells us that the people enthusiastically pitched in and did their part. Goldsmiths, priests, merchants, businessmen, gatekeepers, and even the city councilmen from the various districts of the city worked side by side to raise up the broken-down walls.

Rebuilding the Walls

And isn't that the way it's supposed to be in the body of Christ? Didn't the apostle Paul say... *Christ—from whom the whole body, joined and knit together by what every joint supplies, according to the effective working by which every part does its share, causes growth of the body* (Ephesians 4:15-16)?

Friend, when we determine to be people of excellence, we not only mature in the things of God, but our witness causes growth in the whole body of Christ. As we unite in Him, each one doing our part—each one putting action to our faith—we can make an impact on a world that's seemingly going farther away from God every day. As Paul told us in 1 Timothy 6:11-12... We can fight the good fight of faith, following after righteousness, godliness, faith, love, patience and meekness and we can do our part to turn this world right side up for Christ!

As Nehemiah and the other workers labored from daylight till dark, the rumors that Israel was rebuilding the walls of Jerusalem began to spread throughout the land. When some of the neighboring enemies of Israel heard about it, they flew into a rage. They began to mock Nehemiah, saying, *"Will they revive the stones out of the heaps of the rubbish which are burned* (Nehemiah 4:2 KJV)?" And, *"If even a fox walked along the top of their wall, it would collapse"* (Nehemiah 4:3 TLB)!

But Nehemiah and the children of Israel just kept on piling stone upon stone, and only a few weeks later the walls had been rebuilt to one-half of their original height! When those who had mocked and scorned Nehemiah heard the news, they were scared out of their wits! So, they rounded up all the enemies of Israel—and devised a scheme to lead an army into Jerusalem.

When the people heard about it, they began to pray to the Lord while also guarding the city faithfully. The Bible says

38 | RICHARD ROBERTS

that many worked with one hand, while they held their swords with the other (See Nehemiah 4:17-18). They continued working long hours—from dawn until dark. Nehemiah proudly declared, *"The people had a heart and mind to work"* (Nehemiah 4:6 AMP).

When the walls had been raised, almost to their full height, it didn't take long for Nehemiah's enemies to hatch another desperate plot. They asked Nehemiah to meet with them in a neighboring city, but he sent back a scorching reply: *"I am doing a great work and cannot come down. Why should the work stop while I leave to come down to you"* (Nehemiah 6:3 AMP)?

But those detractors kept begging him to come down from the wall! In fact, they sent that very same message to him four different times!

Now, doesn't that just sound like what the devil does to us? He continually tries to distract us…to try to get us off track, to try to distort God's Word and block us from finishing the work God has called us to do. Only an excellent and determined spirit will help us wave away the distractions and silence the detractors.

In one final, last-ditch effort, Nehemiah's detractors bribed one of the so-called prophets of Jerusalem and told him to give Nehemiah a false prophecy. So, the prophet warned Nehemiah to hide in the temple.

Now you must understand that the Jewish law in those days strictly prohibited anyone except the priests to enter the temple. If someone broke that law, it was a crime which was punishable by death. But, thank God, Nehemiah realized that the prophet's warning was more of the enemy's treachery, and he refused to fall for their trap! (See Nehemiah 6:10-13 TLB.)

In Nehemiah 6:15, the Bible declares that the walls of

Jerusalem were towering over the city, fully completed, **only fifty-two days after they had begun the work**! How on earth did they finish such a monumental project so quickly? Because Nehemiah was a man of excellence, determined to finish the task before him… *"I put all my energy into rebuilding the wall"* (Nehemiah 5:16 GNT)!

When the news spread throughout the land that Jerusalem's walls were standing like a sentinel, tall and proud, the Bible says that Israel's enemies *"realized that they had lost face, since everyone knew that the work had been done with God's help"* (Nehemiah 6:16 GNT).

Not only did Nehemiah and the people accomplish an incredible work for God and not only did they blot out a terrible disgrace from the city of Jerusalem, *but the Lord God of Israel was also glorified in the process!*

Because Nehemiah was of one purpose and one mind and had developed his own spirit of excellence that was within him, he was able to thwart the plans and schemes of the enemy and the distractions they tried to throw his way.

Be a Wall-Builder

I believe this should be the story of our lives as well! Being a people with an excellent spirit means we should square our shoulders, roll up our sleeves, put action to our faith, and work like there's no tomorrow!

We must work to rebuild wherever the walls have been broken down—broken walls of hatred and misunderstanding…the broken walls of family relationships, or of racial injustice—or anywhere the devil may have created a breach in the walls of Christian unity and charity.

There's still a great and mighty work to be done for the Lord, and we must not come down from the wall until it's finished!

CHAPTER 7

Embracing the 2 D's of Excellence— Discipline and Diligence

*I do the very best I know how, the very best I can,
and I mean to keep on doing so until the end.*

ABRAHAM LINCOLN

et's dig a little deeper into God's Word to learn what caused young Daniel to have such an excellent spirit…

In Daniel 1:8, the Bible says that he refused to defile himself by partaking of the king's meat. Why? Because it would have violated the laws of his Jewish faith.

Now that took discipline. That took self-control and determination.

While Daniel was in training to go into service to this

foreign, Gentile king, he was assigned a daily amount of food and wine from the king's table. However, this food and drink was forbidden according to his beliefs, and he resolved not to defile himself with it. (See Daniel 1:5 & 8.)

How was Daniel able to do that? He had disciplined himself to obey the Lord. He knew that to develop an excellent spirit, he had to live a disciplined life.

Not only was Daniel a man of fervent prayer but he was also a tireless worker for the Lord, diligently carrying out his duties and responsibilities as he relied on his faith in the One True God to get him through his captivity.

In James 2:26, the Bible declares that *faith without works is dead.* That means you can pray what would seem like a hole through the sky, but unless you put some action to your faith, not much is likely to happen.

Without discipline in our lives, we'll have disorder, chaos and confusion. And 1 Corinthians 14:33 tells us that *God is not the author of confusion, but of peace.*

When I think about discipline, the first thing that comes to my mind is the rigid discipline that's required for a man or a woman to become a soldier. Didn't the apostle Paul say that as Christians we must "endure hardness, as a good soldier of Jesus Christ" (2 Timothy 2:3)? Well, that's exactly what Daniel did when he refused to defile himself with the king's meat. He was being offered a taste of the good life, but he did not want to defile himself in the sight of God, **so he refused it.**

Paul also said in 2 Timothy 2:4 that no man who goes to war entangles himself with the affairs of this life. God had chosen Daniel and because of his excellent spirit, he refused to get bogged down by any type of behavior that would displease the Lord.

I'm reminded of the story of another soldier in the Bible, a great warrior named David.

David and his men were men of strong discipline, *and they, too, endured hardness!*

Even as a young man, David had disciplined himself to become a worshiper of God and a champion for Him. He had practiced with his slingshot hour after hour as he guarded his father's flocks on the hillsides surrounding Bethlehem. He had worked so long and so hard that he had become a crack shot.

Now that takes discipline! That takes skill! That takes practice and training and diligence! **David was a young man who had discipline in his life.**

So, by the time Goliath, a champion Philistine giant who stood some nine feet tall, started strutting his stuff before the armies of Israel, David had already prepared himself for battle. How? By disciplining himself and giving all diligence to his training with his slingshot. He had already confronted and killed a lion and a bear. Now, this young shepherd boy, armed with only a stick, his slingshot, five smooth stones, and his faith, defeated that godless Philistine giant with one shot to his forehead! (See 1 Samuel chapter 17.)

Later, when God set David upon the throne of Israel, the nation was in total disarray. Israel's former king, Saul, had disobeyed the Lord and had put the entire country in jeopardy, leaving them exposed to violent attacks from their enemies.

But David, with his discipline—his grit and determination and his spirit of excellence—ascended to the throne and began to drive the enemies of Israel from her borders. Then he went on to conquer the bordering nations, creating a buffer zone between Israel and her enemies.

If you look at the picture the Bible paints for us of David's mighty men, you can see that they were extremely well disciplined, also. First Chronicles 12:2 declares, *They were armed with bows, and could use both the right hand and the left in hurling stones and shooting arrows.* I mean, that takes discipline. It's the same kind of discipline that drives an athlete to train for excellence in his or her sport.

Another verse tells us that some of David's fighting men *had faces like that of a lion and were as swift as gazelles...the least of them was a match for a hundred and the greatest for a thousand* (1 Chronicles 12:8 & 14). Those men were finely tuned, highly trained men of war! *Just imagine standing eyeball to eyeball with men whose faces were like the faces of lions!*

First Chronicles 12:32 tells us that another particular group of David's warriors were *men that had understanding of the times, to know what Israel ought to do.*

Believe me, it takes a disciplined spirit to have an understanding of the times so you can know how to lead people in the right direction.

So, David's men not only disciplined their spirits to face the battles of life like lions, but they also disciplined their minds to have the wisdom to know what Israel ought to do. Those warriors disciplined their spirits, minds, and bodies!

The Bible tells us that the men of Zebulun who fought with David were *expert in war, with all instruments of war, fifty thousand, which could keep rank: they were not of double heart* (1 Chronicles 12:33). Now, fifty thousand men is a whole lot of men to be able to stay in rank. That means not a single soldier broke rank! How could they maintain that kind of discipline? The Scripture gives us the answer when it says, "They were not of double heart." *They were single-minded about their duty to making David king and to God.*

A SPIRIT OF EXCELLENCE | 45

But I believe one of the most revealing statements the Bible makes about David's men is found in I Chronicles 12:38: *All these men of war... came with a perfect heart.* David's warriors were so highly disciplined that their hearts were in tune with one another. There was a unity of spirit among them.

Jesus prayed that all believers might become as one, just as He and God are one. (See John 17:11.) That's how it's supposed to be with us as Christians when we stand shoulder to shoulder, arm in arm, united for the cause of Christ.

Friend, there's an appalling lack of discipline in the world today. And there's also a lack of discipline in the body of Christ today.

On many fronts, because the truth of God's Word is not being preached and therefore practiced, instead of developing people who have excellent spirits, we're developing people who don't even know the meaning of—let alone the worth of—the words *discipline, diligence or excellence.* They equate those words with some type of outdated religious bondage. But discipline isn't oppression and it isn't a burden*! For the time being no discipline brings joy, but seems sad and painful; yet to those who have been trained by it, afterwards it yields the peaceful fruit of righteousness [right standing with God and a lifestyle and attitude that seeks conformity to God's will and purpose]* (Hebrews 12:11 AMP).

Excellence isn't developed without discipline and diligence. They are absolutely vital attributes for the body of Christ to have to become a people of excellence. As ministers of the Gospel and as soldiers of the cross, we must have discipline in our lives. **True biblical discipline will produce true freedom in your life!**

It takes discipline to confront life's battles with backbone and intestinal fortitude. It takes discipline to keep from quivering in fear when the devil roars up and shakes his fist in your face. It takes discipline to square your shoulders and take on the brutal giants of this life.

I remember watching a movie one time about Geronimo, the well-known chief of the Native American Apache nation. He was a fierce leader who did everything in his power to defend the land which he believed to be his own.

It is said that Geronimo and the band of men who traveled with him were some of the world's toughest guerrilla fighters. When they crossed the desert, they could seemingly disappear into the landscape. They could race for miles without breaking a sweat.

I once heard that the Apache brave's prayer was this: "Give me another enemy, because my enemies make me strong."

You may be thinking, *Richard, what does that have to do with you and me today?*

It means that **the battles of life can make us strong… strong in our attitude about life, strong in our willingness to go the extra mile…and strong in our faith!**

My father taught me that in life, I would face many battles. And how I handled the battles would help make or break my life. But, it seems as if many Christians have allowed the devil to bully them into falling to pieces every time he launches an attack. However, Ephesians 6:16 assures us that when we hold up the shield of faith, we are able to quench all the fiery darts of the wicked one.

And in Joshua 1:9 we're encouraged… *"Be strong and of good courage; do not be afraid, nor be dismayed, for the Lord your God is with you wherever you go."*

I challenge you today to endure hardness as a good soldier of the cross. Develop strong discipline in your life, and don't shrink from the battles that loom before you. ***Stand your ground, and let the Lord complete the good work that He's begun in you!*** If you will, I believe that those "enemies" you've been frightened of are the very things that will make you strong and help you develop your own excellent spirit!

CHAPTER 8

Reigning in Life and
Triumphing over Adversity

If a man is called to be a street sweeper, he should sweep the streets even as Michelangelo painted or as Beethoven wrote music or Shakespeare wrote poetry. He should sweep streets so well that all the hosts of Heaven and earth shall pause to say, "Here lived a great street sweeper who did his job well."

MARTIN LUTHER KING, JR.

There is another story of a man in the Bible who, like Daniel, was unflinchingly loyal to the Lord in spite of Satan's cruel strategies. I'm talking about the story of Job.

The account of Job in the Bible tells us that he was a man of means; *the greatest man among all the people of the East.* He was said to be...*blameless and upright; fearing God and shunning evil.*

Job had seven sons and three daughters, owned 7,000 sheep, 3,000 camels, 500 yoke of oxen and 500 donkeys—and a large number of helpers! He was a man of great wealth who lived a life of luxury.

Then one day, in one fleeting moment, rustlers swept down from the north and stole all of his camels, oxen and donkeys. Then a fire burned up his flocks of sheep as well as his servants.

Next, a cyclone swept in from the desert and smashed his oldest son's house to the ground, killing all ten of his children.

And if that wasn't enough, the Bible goes on to record that after all that had happened, *Satan afflicted Job with painful sores from the soles of his feet to the top of his head.*

Oh my word! How much can one person endure?

But the Bible says… *At this, Job got up and tore his robe and shaved his head. Then he fell to the ground in worship and said: "Naked I came from my mother's womb, and naked I will depart. The Lord gave and the Lord has taken away; may the name of the Lord be praised."* **In all this**, *Job did not sin by charging God with wrongdoing* (Job 1:20-22 NIV).

Wow! Could this be said of any of us if the same or a similar thing happened in our lives?

Staying the Course

It's pretty easy to be loyal to God when everything is going our way and running like clockwork. It's another thing when the bottom falls out from under us.

How do we maintain our faith when facing the loss of everything we hold dear? How do we not place blame on God when evil things are spoken to us and about us? How do we remain a person of integrity and excellence when we've been diagnosed with a terminal disease? How do we not turn inward or strike out at others when we ourselves have been used and abused?

I'm sure, like Job, we would be totally devastated. And I certainly do not have all the answers for when bad things happen to good people.

But having experienced my own share of pain and heartache, I know and can declare without hesitation that my God is faithful.

The Bible talks about suffering in 2 Corinthians 1:3-5 (from *The Message*)…

All praise to the God and Father of our Master, Jesus the Messiah! Father of all mercy! God of all healing counsel! He comes alongside us when we go through hard times, and before you know it, he brings us alongside someone else who is going through hard times so that we can be there for that person just as God was there for us. We have plenty of hard times that come from following the Messiah, but no more so than the good times of his healing comfort—we get a full measure of that, too.

This entire book is about learning how we can become a person of excellence. Dealing with sorrow or hardship is something most of us will probably have to do at some point along this journey called the road of life. Our faith will be tried and put under pressure by the trials of life.

But in James 1:2-4, he encourages us with these words (again from *The Message*)…

Consider it a sheer gift, friends, when tests and challenges come at you from all sides. You know that under pressure, your faith-life is forced into the open and shows its true colors. So don't try to get out of anything prematurely. Let it do its work so you become mature and well-developed, not deficient in any way.

And in Romans 5:1-5, the apostle Paul, in talking about our faith triumphing over troubles, writes…

…but we also glory in tribulations, knowing that tribulation produces perseverance; and perseverance, character; and character [excellence of spirit], *hope. Now hope does not disappoint, because the love of God has been poured out in our hearts by the Holy Spirit who was given to us.*

We are not guaranteed a bed of roses after we accept Christ as Savior. But we are promised that God will never leave us or forsake us, and He will either lead us through every trial or He will carry us through them to the other side. *God always causes us to triumph in Christ* (2 Corinthians 2:14 KJV).

Yes, Job remained loyal to the Lord even when he was afflicted and brought low, forsaken by his friends. His own wife even told him he should just curse God and die. But, through everything, Job proclaimed, "God, even if You slay me, yet will I trust in You!"

He was really saying, "No matter what happens, no matter whether there is sunshine or rain, no matter whether the skies are blue or gray, I'm going on with the Lord!"

And… this is not the end of Job's story! God rewarded his loyalty—his excellence of spirit—by blessing him doubly! Chapter 42, verse 12, says… *The Lord blessed the latter part of Job's life more than the first* [seven more sons and three more daughters, plus more livestock than he had previously]. *After this, Job lived a hundred and forty years; he saw his children and their children to the fourth generation. And so he died, old and full of years.*

Friend, you are not defined by what you are going through

or what has happened to you in the past. God knows the beginning to the end of your life, and it's not over until He says it over. No matter the struggle, the heartache, the physical or mental disability, the color of your skin, your age, your gender or your station in life, God has a great plan for your life and He will perfect that plan and bring it to fruition, as you trust Him and yield yourself to Him (Psalm 138:8). You are valuable, you are loved, and you have an honored place in His kingdom.

CHAPTER 9

Loyalty Brings Reward

Always let others see you behaving properly, even though they may still accuse you of doing wrong. Then on the day of judgment, they will honor God by telling the good things they saw you do.

1 PETER 2:12 CEV

I was raised by my father and mother to be loyal to the Lord. I thank God that He has helped me remain loyal to Him even during the most gut-wrenching trials of my life.

I'll never forget the night I stood in an intensive care unit in a hospital here in Tulsa, Oklahoma, and watched doctors make an incision in my little newborn boy's chest. They struggled desperately to make his lungs start breathing again, but it was all to no avail.

Lindsay and I had already suffered through several miscarriages and when little Richard Oral slipped away to be with Jesus, everybody in that room was staring at me. They knew that I was a healing evangelist, the son of a man whose name is synonymous with healing. But my little boy had just died in my arms, and everybody wanted to know what I would do next.

Through my tears and anguish, I cried out to the Lord with the loudest voice I could muster, and I shouted, "Lord, though You slay me, yet will I trust in You!"

Now, I never would have tried to make a deal with God for my son's life. I never would have said something like, "Lord, if You will heal my boy, then I'll do such and such." Why? Because I knew that God knew something about Richard Oral's death that I didn't know, and I had made up my mind to trust Him and to be loyal to the Lord with no strings attached.

When I said, "God, though You slay me, yet will I trust in You," I had no idea that our daughter Jordan would come into the world a little more than a year later. I had no idea that God would give us our other two precious daughters, Olivia and Chloe. I had no way of knowing that He would reward my loyalty by blessing Lindsay and me with more children. All I knew was this: I was prepared to serve the Lord **NO MATTER WHAT!**

Now perhaps you're thinking, *Richard, hasn't there ever been a time when you've been tempted to be disloyal?*

Of course, there have been moments in my life when I've been tempted to betray the Lord. No doubt we've all had times when we've been in so much despair that it would have been easy to sell out our loyalty. But I've made up my mind that I'm not going to be an empty shell of a Christian. I'm going to follow in the footsteps of my Savior. *I'm going to be loyal to my heavenly Father NO MATTER WHAT!*

A SPIRIT OF EXCELLENCE | 57

And, friend, you can determine to do the same. The Bible says in Joshua 24:15 KJV… *Choose you this day whom ye will serve…but as for me and my house, we will serve the Lord.*

Make a determination of your faith TODAY that you will be a person of loyalty to God…a person of excellence.

CHAPTER 10

Free, Indeed

And the LORD *will make you the head and not the tail; you shall be above only, and not be beneath, if you heed the commandments of the* LORD *your God.*

DEUTERONOMY 28:13

Let me bring Daniel's story to a climax by telling you that above all else, Daniel was a man who believed God. He was a man of faith, and his faith caused him to look up to the limitless, incomparable Lord and BELIEVE.

Not only was he a man of prayer, a man of work, and a man of discipline, but he also, as did Nehemiah and Job, remained loyal to the Lord.

So, let me ask you… Do you believe God today?

In the midst of all the trials you may be going through… the endless struggle to overcome the guilt from all the baggage you've been dragging around from your past, **do you still**

believe God can work in you and through you? YES, He can…and He wants to!

Is there something that has you bound and shackled, and you're not really sure if God can set you free?

I challenge you today to choose to believe God. John 8:36 says… *If the Son makes you free, you shall be free indeed.* God sent His Son to save you and to give you abundant life in Him.

Oh, I know it's so easy to focus in on all that's going on around you and on the circumstances that you may find yourself in. It's so easy to be distracted when all you hear on a daily basis are grim predictions about the future! And you may have tried to change on your own many times before and failed. *But God…*

I want to encourage you with the fact that God loves you…He's for you, not against you…He has a good plan for your life and He cares about you in the "right now" of your life. Not to mention getting to spend eternity with Him in Heaven!

You are not an accident… You are not unwanted or unloved… You do have the potential to be all God called you to be, and you can rise up to be a person of excellence.

Don't give up! It's never too late when God is in it. Begin to put Him first in every aspect of your life and then believe and expect Him to bring about a turnaround in your life. He is faithful and He will honor you as you honor Him.

CHAPTER 11

For Such a Time as This

Yet indeed I also count all things loss for the excellence of the knowledge of Christ Jesus my Lord, for whom I have suffered the loss of all things, and count them as rubbish, that I may gain Christ.

PHILIPPIANS 3:8

I have one more example to share with you…and this one is of a great woman of the Bible who also had an excellent spirit. Her name was Esther.

In the third year of his reign, King Xerxes gave a banquet for all his nobles and officials. At the same time, Queen Vashti also gave a banquet for the women in the royal palace.

On the seventh day of the celebration, the king sent for the queen so that he might display her beauty to the people and nobles. But, Queen Vashti refused to come. The king burned with anger against the queen. So, the king put forth a decree that the queen should never again enter the presence of the king and was advised to give her royal position to someone else who was better.

A search was then made for all the most beautiful girls to come into the harem of the king. They were to be treated with beauty treatments and given special food for twelve months.

Now, Esther, a Jewish exile of the tribe of Benjamin, had been brought to live with her Uncle Mordecai, who served the king, after her father and mother died. *The young woman was lovely and beautiful* (Esther 2:7). She, too, was brought into the king's harem; however, she had been instructed by her uncle never to reveal her nationality and family background.

Finally, the day came for her to be taken to the king, and she won his favor and approval more than any of the other girls, and the king made Esther his queen.

Now, the king had a high noble by the name of Haman, and the king had commanded all the other royal officials to kneel down and pay honor to him. However, Mordecai, being a Jew, refused to bow down. This enraged Haman—not only against Mordecai, but he sought to destroy all of Mordecai's people, the Jews, throughout the kingdom. He even promised to put ten thousand talents of silver into the royal treasury for the men who would carry out his plan.

So, Haman went to the king, saying in essence, "There are people in the provinces of your kingdom who don't obey your laws, and it's not in your best interest to tolerate them." He asked for a decree to be issued to have all the Jews in the land destroyed and the king agreed. Dispatches were sent out with the order to destroy, kill and annihilate all the Jews—young and old, women and children—in a single day.

A SPIRIT OF EXCELLENCE | **63**

When Mordecai and the Jewish people learned of this decree, there was great mourning with fasting, weeping and wailing.

Mordecai got word to Esther to urge her to go into the king's presence to beg for mercy and plead with him for her people. But you see, for those who approached the king without being summoned first, there was but one law…they must be put to death. The only exception was that if the king extended his gold scepter to that person, their life would be spared.

Esther reported this fact to Mordecai and he replied, "Don't think because you're in the palace that you'll be spared. If you remain silent, you and your family will perish. *Yet who knows whether you have come to the kingdom for such a time as this"?* (See Esther 4:13-14.)

I want to stop right here and say that sometimes, we may find ourselves in the midst of circumstances which we don't understand. We wonder why God doesn't just intervene and do something!

I believe that because we have God's excellent spirit within us, we are sometimes put into these times and situations to be a positive influence for the good He is trying to accomplish. Yes, of course, God is sovereign and He can do anything. But He works in the hearts, minds and spirits of His people. And if we are willing and obedient to stay the course and see His plan and purpose worked out, we will reap the rewards and He will be glorified in the process.

So, Esther agreed to do it and said, "If I perish, I perish."

She put on her royal robes and went into the inner court of the palace. The king saw her and, being pleased to see her, held out the gold scepter to her. He asked her what her request was and offered to give her "up to half of the kingdom." She revealed her heritage and made her request known to the king, asking that her life and the lives of her people be spared. She explained that Haman had asked for this evil decree because of his hatred for Mordecai and the king was furious. Haman and his sons were taken to the gallows that he had prepared for Mordecai and were hanged on it. His signet ring was given to Mordecai and he was made second in rank to the king. He had the dispatches that Haman had sent out for the destruction of the Jews revoked and a new edict was written and granted, saying the Jews in every city had the right to assemble and protect themselves.

To this day, devout Jews still observe the feast of Purim to celebrate their deliverance from destruction when Queen Esther chose to exercise her excellent spirit and defy the king, in spite of her fear or the consequences.

Friend, fear is a strong emotion that can sometimes immobilize us, make us doubt God, and keep us from moving forward. Fear is a spiritual scare tactic of the devil. It originates from him and if we listen to his lies and let fear grow in us, it can shut us down in our tracks.

But 2 Timothy 1:7 tells us… *For God has not given us a spirit of fear, but of power and of love and of a sound mind.*

Did you get that? As a child of God…

You have POWER…*But you shall receive power when the Holy Spirit has come upon you* (Acts 1:8).

You have LOVE… *The love of God has been poured out in our hearts by the Holy Spirit who was given to us* (Romans 5:5).

You have a SOUND MIND… *But he who is spiritual judges all things, yet he himself is rightly judged by no one… But we have the mind of Christ* (1 Corinthians 2:15-16).

And since Acts 10:34 tells us that God is no respecter of persons, if we'll trust God and allow Him to work—even when we're fearful, we can show that same spirit of excellence that Esther displayed and see miraculous change!

Summary

Friend, I don't believe you're reading this book by accident… God has called you to live a life of excellence in Him, and I believe you and God had a divine appointment to meet this very hour!

And I want to encourage you that if you don't know Jesus as your personal Lord and Savior, if you've never asked Him into your heart and life, then this is your hour to be saved, to be healed, to be filled with the power of God's Spirit!

Oh, you may know a lot *about* this Man called Jesus, and you may have read the Bible from cover to cover, but you may not *know* the God of the Bible. Or perhaps your heart was once stirred by the Lord, and you had a heartfelt experience with Him, but now you've slipped away, and your heart has grown cold. Praise God, today is your day to make a fresh, new commitment to Jesus!

Today—right now—if you would like to take your place in God's kingdom, I invite you to pray the prayer below. God loves you. You are of great worth and value to Him. He gave

His Son, Jesus, to die for you so you could live an abundant and excellent life.

O God, be merciful to me, a sinner, a backslider. Forgive me of my sins, and give me a salvation that I can feel down in my soul. I receive You as my Savior, my Healer, my Deliverer, and the One Who died on the Cross to purchase these things for me. From this hour, I will live to serve You, with all my whole heart and all my strength. I'll take my stand for the things that Heaven stands for— Your Word and Your truth. Thank You for coming into my heart, and I believe I'll never be the same again! In the mighty Name of Jesus, I pray. Amen.

Now, if you prayed that prayer, I have a little booklet I'd like to send you, called ***How to Live Your New Life.*** You can get a copy by calling 918-495-7777 or visiting my website RichardRoberts.org.

And I encourage you to attend a strong Bible-believing church where like-minded believers can help you mature and grow in the knowledge of the Lord.

I pray that the stories, examples and insight from my own life experiences which I've shared with you in this book will inspire you to continually do your best to be a person of excellent spirit. I believe that as you do, you will see God's promises for you come to pass in your life, just as Joshua 1:8 says… *This Book of the Law* [God's Word] *shall not depart from your mouth, but you shall meditate in it day and night, that you may observe to do according to all that is written in it. For then you will make your way prosperous, and then you will have good success.*

I want to pray for you…

Father, on this day I pray my reader will make a bold and courageous decision to develop the excellent spirit which You have birthed in them. I pray that they will diligently seek Your face and not just Your hand. I pray that they will become a person of strong discipline and a person for whom You can say, "My precious child. Not only do they have great faith, but they possess an excellent spirit." In the name of Jesus, I pray. Amen.

For prayer, call

The Abundant Life Prayer Group at

918-495-7777,

or contact us online at

www.RichardRoberts.org

RICHARD ROBERTS

Richard Roberts, B.A., M.A., D.Min., is the Chairman and CEO of Richard Roberts Ministries and has dedicated his life to ministering the saving, healing, delivering power of Jesus Christ around the world.

Richard has ministered God's healing power in 39 nations spanning six continents. In his healing outreaches, Richard has ministered to crowds of over 200,000 people in a single service. His services are marked with supernatural miracles and healings and by a tremendous move of the Spirit. Today, Richard focuses on his *Greater Works* international pastors conferences where he teaches and trains pastors in underdeveloped nations to take the full gospel with miracles, healing and signs following to their villages, cities, and nations, as Jesus said in John 14:12.

Richard and his wife, Lindsay, also host *The Place for Miracles*—a half-hour inspirational TV broadcast that reaches out to millions worldwide. Together, Richard and Lindsay minister in the power of the Holy Spirit, praying for those who need a miracle of healing in some area of their lives.

In 2010, Richard founded the *Richard Roberts School of Miracles* which offers online Bible courses to help equip Christians with practical, hands-on experience in applying God's Word and His healing power in their own lives and in the lives of others, especially emphasizing how Christians can enjoy a life empowered by the Holy Spirit.

In addition, Richard hosts a weekly podcast, *Expect a Miracle*, with fascinating in-depth interviews with pastors, ministers and Christian leaders. He has also authored a number of publications and other inspirational material, including ...*Your Road to a Better Life, Unstoppable Increase, He's A Healing Jesus, Thrive—Eliminating Lack from Your Life, God's Healing Touch*...and more!